Original title:
Words Among the Willows

Copyright © 2025 Creative Arts Management OÜ
All rights reserved.

Author: Christian Leclair
ISBN HARDBACK: 978-1-80567-448-1
ISBN PAPERBACK: 978-1-80567-747-5

Whispers Beneath the Canopy

Under leaves, laughter hides,
Squirrels gossip, no one bides.
The raccoons chuckle, what a show,
As owls roll eyes, they steal the glow.

A crow critiques the blushing sun,
While rabbits hop, it's all in fun.
Dancing shadows, a playful tease,
Nature giggles in the breeze.

Secrets in the Tree Shadows

In shadows deep, secrets lie,
A frog sings low, oh, my, oh my!
The breeze tells tales, all absurd,
Of a snail who thinks he's really a bird.

Chipmunks debate who's the fastest,
Who knew nature was such a blast?
With whispers that tickle, and branches that sway,
The forest's a stage, come out and play.

Echoes of the Whispering Breeze

The wind sneezes, trees do shake,
Is it just me, or did they quake?
Cicadas giggle, ready to tease,
While dandelions dance with ease.

A wise old oak takes a deep breath,
Claiming he's seen it all—life and death.
But the blades just laugh, "An old tree's prank!"
And the whispers of greenery fill the tank.

Stories Written in the Bark

Carved in bark, a tale unfolds,
Of a turtle who thought he was bold.
The wise old tree shakes its head,
Says, 'Slow and steady's a story misread.'

Branches gossip, roots intertwine,
While the lizards sunbathe, feeling divine.
Each knot holds laughter, a flicker of joy,
In the forest's charm, every critter's a ploy.

Reflections on the Roots of Remembrance

In the grove where whispers play,
Squirrels dance in bright array.
Leaves chuckle high up in the breeze,
While ants host tea under the trees.

Branches twist with a silent cheer,
As I trip over roots that appear.
A chipmunk giggles, oh so sly,
Saying, 'Hey buddy, watch you fly!'

The bark holds tales of blooming jest,
Of acorns that put on a quest.
The sun winks down, a playful tease,
As clouds make faces, just to please.

Upon the grass, I pose with flair,
A beetle's laugh fills the air.
I join the jest, with a spin and twirl,
As nature giggles, life's a whirl.

Harmonies from the Hidden Haven

In a nook where shadows sway,
Frogs croak out their cabaret.
Owls hoot jokes that never land,
While turtles discuss the latest band.

Pinecones drop like audience claps,
As rabbits laugh in funny caps.
A breeze brings giggles, soft and light,
As daisies bloom in pure delight.

A fox prances like a showman bold,
Wearing stories that never get old.
With every rustle, a chuckle grows,
In this haven where laughter flows.

The melodies twist through bark and leaves,
Planting silliness one believes.
Nature sings, oh what a thrill!
In the hidden haven, joy's the drill.

Ruminations in the Rustling Grasses

In the breeze, the tall grass quakes,
Whispers of secrets that nature makes.
Frogs croak like they're telling a joke,
While crickets chirp in their fine bespoke.

Bumblebees buzz with a purpose so grand,
Chasing daisies just like a band.
Ants march in lines, a tiny parade,
While a worm serves as a mild charade.

Echoed Memories under the Elder Trees

Under the branches where shadows play,
Old stories dance in a funny way.
Squirrels gossip in their nutty slurs,
While owls hoot jokes without any slurs.

Rabbits laugh at their own pure grace,
Hopping along with a wobbly pace.
The wind carries giggles through the leaves,
As nature herself plots schemes and thieves.

Musings on the Mellowed Moss

On a bed of green with a spongy feel,
Fungi giggle, 'This is the deal!'
Sloths hang low with a lazy grin,
Playing chess with the moss, they win.

A chipmunk juggles seeds with delight,
While the sun sets low, painting skies bright.
Beneath the fuzzy, the critters conspire,
Tickling the ground as they dance to a choir.

Parables of the Placid Ponds

Reflective waters, a mirror so bright,
Where frogs wear crowns, feeling quite right.
Turtles float by with their tired smiles,
Plotting their journeys, crossing countless miles.

A duck quacks loudly, a comedic thud,
While fish swim by, avoiding the mud.
Nature's stage, with slapstick aplomb,
As laughter ripples, our troubles are gone.

Tales from the Twisted Trunks

Beneath the branches, squirrels tease,
While owls hoot tales with utmost ease.
A raccoon claims the crown of leaves,
Sipping acorns like a king who grieves.

A fox tells jokes to a passing hare,
Who laughs so hard, he nearly tears!
With every line, the forest cheers,
As night draws near, no room for fears.

Lullabies of the Leafy Labyrinth

In cozy nooks where crickets hum,
A sleepy snail plays the drum.
The hedgehogs waltz with grace and might,
While fireflies twinkle, bright as light.

A sleepy bear gets lost in dreams,
Chasing fish, or so it seems.
With giggles echoing in the air,
The forest sings without a care.

Sonnets by the Silken Streams

The fish are gossiping, or so it's said,
While frogs throw shade from their mossy bed.
The reeds are dancing, swaying low,
To the rhythm of the flowing flow.

A turtle recites with a slow-paced rhyme,
Claiming he's the greatest, given the time.
But the water striders just roll their eyes,
As the sun sets low in a laughing guise.

Rhythms of the Rustic Roots

The path is paved with acorn pies,
Where bumblebees wear silly ties.
A raccoon shows off his clumsy dance,
While the trees sway in a merry prance.

The mushrooms giggle, hats askew,
As ladybugs take a curtsy queue.
With every crinkle, the forest plays,
In a world of joy where laughter stays.

Brief Histories of Swaying Shoots

Little shoots sway with delight,
They gossip 'til the fall of night.
The breeze is a stand-up comic here,
Tickling leaves, spreading cheer.

A butterfly flaps, what a sight,
Spilling secrets, taking flight.
Roots shrug off a muddy joke,
While clouds chuckle, as they poke.

Rabbits listening with big, round ears,
Chime in, sharing laughter and cheers.
Nearby, a squirrel spins a tale,
Of acorns dropping like a fail.

Whispers rustle among the grass,
As if the trees all shared a class.
They teach the art of jest and fun,
In their leafy kingdom, they've won.

An Ode to Rustling Tales

Amid the trees, a chorus sings,
Of mischief, laughter, silly things.
The branches dance, a merry show,
As breezes nudge them to and fro.

A crow caws loud, a rascal bold,
Claiming tales of treasures untold.
The owls hoot in wise disdain,
While crickets join the ribald strain.

A raccoon sneaks with crafty flair,
Snatching snacks from unaware air.
Vines twist up, like wagging tongues,
In the land where laughter thrives and stuns.

With every rustle, a giggle shared,
Nature crafts tales where all are dared.
Let's join the revel in wild delight,
As stories flutter in the warm moonlight.

Inklings Beneath the Branches

Beneath the boughs, ideas sprout,
With giggles echoing all about.
A chipmunk scribbles on a leaf,
Joking of squirrels, light-hearted mischief.

The clever beetle knows the score,
Creeping close for a laugh encore.
While ladybugs roll, in pure delight,
Under the sun, looking quite bright.

Each twig and twig is a storyteller,
With antics that could make a feller.
A tree frog croaks with comedic timing,
In the forest stage, their rhythm climbing.

Every dewdrop holds a spark,
Of tales that wander, never dark,
In a world where whimsy takes flight,
Where each leaf tells stories, day and night.

Nature's Subtle Ink

With ink made of sap, tales run,
Of leaf and branch, of mirth and fun.
The forest floor is a canvas wide,
Where laughter blooms and hugs reside.

A skunk in stripes prances about,
Telling jokes, shouting, "No doubt!"
While moles dig deep with grinning glee,
Crafting puns in the root-tangled spree.

The wind plays tricks, an artist free,
Brushing the leaves, painting with glee.
As fawns prance in their woodland class,
Learning the art of the odd and brash.

In every whisper, a chuckle glows,
Nature's humor cleverly flows.
So heed the tales in each gentle breeze,
Where laughter dances among the trees.

Murmurs of the Misty Meadow

In a field where daisies dance,
Squirrels gossip, pigs prance,
Hares hold court, all in jest,
Who can hop the highest? A quest!

Butterflies are busy boasting,
At the nectar, they are toasting.
Bees compete in buzzing tunes,
While the grass hums old cartoons.

A raccoon steals a picnic pie,
While the skunks all swoon and sigh.
Laughter echoes near the brook,
As frogs recite a silly book.

Mushrooms giggle in the shade,
Trading tales of plans they've made.
Every critter finds a way,
To turn a dull into a play.

Phrases in the Petals' Embrace

Petals whisper secrets sweet,
As ants shuffle on their feet.
Bumblebees recount their trips,
Outrageous tales from flower lips.

"Look at me!" cries dandelion,
Playing tricks, its roots defying.
Tulips join with a cheeky grin,
"Let's play hide and seek in the bin!"

A ladybug donned in red,
Tells of dreams and thoughts she's bred.
Shealily rolls, then spins around,
While laughter bubbles from the ground.

Butterflies exchange fashion tips,
With the boldest amongst the quips.
Nature's chat is never dull,
In colors bright, they pull and cull.

Ballads in the Breezy Boughs

Up high where the branches sway,
Birds hold concerts every day.
Chirps and trills become a song,
A melody where all belong.

Crows boast tales of nighttime haps,
While squirrels chuckle, sharing slaps.
A woodpecker taps out a rhyme,
In sync with nature's grand time.

A wise old owl sneaks in a pun,
"Who's afraid of the scary sun?"
Marshes croak with froggy cheer,
While the breeze spreads joy far and near.

Winds provide a playful breeze,
Rustling leaves, a ruckus with ease.
Nature hums a merry tune,
Underneath the chuckling moon.

Chronicles of the Charmed Canopy

Under the shade, a table set,
With acorns, nuts, and none regret.
Rabbits dine on leafy greens,
While the chipmunks plan their scenes.

"Let's start a band!" a sparrow cries,
"It will be fun beneath the skies!"
With twig guitars, they form a crew,
All the trees sway with laughter too.

A fox juggles with fallen fruits,
While raccoons grasp sticky roots.
Squirrels recite old legends bold,
Of hidden treasures and riches told.

The moon peeks in, a curious guest,
To witness nature's wild fest.
With glee, they spin till night's embrace,
In a woodland wonderland of grace.

Hymns of the Leafy Arch

Beneath the canopy so vast,
A squirrel's chat goes by so fast.
With acorns dear, he plots and schemes,
His heist is made of daring dreams.

A ladybug with polka dots,
Claims she's a queen, and never rots.
The grasshoppers dance, a cheerful bunch,
While frogs croak out a lunch-time crunch.

The whispers rustle through the trees,
As gossip spreads upon the breeze.
A rabbit's sigh, a moment glum,
His carrot stash is all just crumbs.

In this green realm of cheer and jest,
Nature's creatures seem truly blessed.
With laughter ringing 'round the bark,
The leafy arch, a playful spark.

Ponderings of a Nature Seeker

Amidst the blooms, one finds a bee,
In search of nectar, full of glee.
He buzzes loud, a tiny cheer,
What's a flower but a banquet dear?

An owl thinks deep, the night is long,
He starts to compose a bedtime song.
With hoots and howls, he sets the stage,
A wise old sage, or just a page?

A chipmunk's stash of nuts and seeds,
A mystery, driven by his needs.
But if he grins with all his might,
Did he just take a rogue nut bite?

So roam the trails, and ponder still,
What secrets hide beyond the hill?
Nature's whimsy knows no end,
Just listen close, it's your best friend.

Lexicon of the Lush Land

In this land of vibrant hues,
A tree with gossip's busy muse.
It chats of robins and their tunes,
While sunlight bathes the laughing dunes.

A bumblebee with dreams so grand,
Is writing novels 'bout the land.
Each petal dances, sways, and swoops,
While ants march by in silly groups.

A toad in love, what a silly sight,
Croaks verses sweet in soft moonlight.
His froggy heart beats brave and true,
For every bug is now a muse!

So come, dear friend, and take a glance,
At nature's odd and merry dance.
With tales of laughter, here we stand,
A lexicon so brightly planned.

Chronicles of the Blooming Fronds

In ferns that sway with stories bold,
   Lie chronicles of laughter told.
   A mockingbird in uproar sings,
Announcing all the joy spring brings.

A hedgehog prances, quills on show,
   His dance a blend of fast and slow.
The mushrooms laugh, 'We're here to stay!'
   In wiggly green, they join the play.

A chip of bark, a tale unfolds,
   The gentle wind its secret holds.
   A flower blushes, sweetly shy,
What will the bees do when they fly?

So gather round, both small and tall,
   Nature's wonders, here for all.
In fronds that bloom, let laughter reign,
   A chronicle of joy, no strain.

Dialogues of Dappled Light

A squirrel named Fred, so spry and spry,
Chased his own tail as he leapt for the sky.
The sun gave a wink, then ducked for a laugh,
While birds chirped out stories of Fred's silly path.

The shadows were giggling, no doubt they had heard,
How Fred tried to dance without missing a word.
A breeze whispered softly, 'Oh, give that a try!'
But Fred just kept spinning, too dizzy to fly.

Verses Carried by the Stream

A fish in the stream wore a bright polka dot,
It swam with such flair, it was quite a hot shot.
The frogs leaped for joy with a ribbit and croak,
While turtles just chuckled, 'Did you see that bloke?'

The water's a stage, where the catfish regales,
With tales of the creek and its unending trails.
They splashed and they laughed, the current a tease,
As minnows danced quickly, 'Hey, catch us if you please!'

Reflections in the Leafy Tangle

In a tangle of leaves, a rabbit took pause,
He pondered his life with a comic kind of awe.
'What's this new diet? It's just grass and field!
I dream of a carrot, please, fate be sealed!'

A nearby owl hooted, 'You really must try,
To hop with great gusto, and reach for the sky!'
But the rabbit just chuckled, 'I think I will pass,
My neighbors seem tastier, I'll munch on some grass.'

The Poetry of Branches

The branches babbled gossip, as leaves danced around,
'Did you see the young nutter who fell to the ground?'
They swayed in delight, with their rustling cheer,
While the squirrels rolled laughter from high up in the sphere.

The sunbeams chimed in, a bright merry cheer,
'Oh, who needs a stage, when the forest's right here?'
They twinkled with joy, making light of the scene,
As shadows and laughter made a perfect serene.

Mosaics of the Wind's Dialogue

In the field, the breeze does play,
Chasing leaves in a wobbly ballet.
A squirrel sneezes, it startles a crow,
As giggles escape from below.

Dandelions dance with a ticklish gleam,
To the rhythm of whispers, a silly theme.
The grasshopper hops, a jester's delight,
His leaps causing laughter with all of his might.

The sun winks down, a cheeky old chap,
A butterfly stumbles, right into a lap.
"Oh, pardon me!" cries the clumsy spree,
As flowers chuckle, "That's just how we be!"

Paths twine and twist with jokes to unwind,
As nature chuckles, a humor divine.
The wind weaves tales, both odd and absurd,
In this funny realm, all senses are stirred.

Revelations in the Rustic Pathways

Down the lane where the daisies bloom,
A goat munches loudly, raising the room.
A rooster crows at the crack of a joke,
His feathers ruffled, the punchline awoke.

A rabbit hops past in a furious dash,
Chasing a butterfly, giving a splash.
"Oh dear!" says the flower, "Can't you all see?
We're just trying to sip it, don't ruffle the spree!"

The logs in the creek chuckle and roll,
"Why so serious? Let's deepen the stroll!"
The tadpoles are giggling in a watery ballet,
As nature enacts its quirky cabaret.

With every twist, the giggles expand,
Even the trees join in the grand stand.
As we wander through laughter, each step we take,
We find joy where the silly winds break.

The Quiet Symphony of the Trees

In the forest, a giggle escapes,
From the shade, where the sly owl gapes.
Branches sway with a whispering grin,
As birds crack jokes, let the fun begin!

The pines hum softly, a playful tune,
While critters tumble like leaves in June.
"Why did you stop?" asks a curious bug,
"Just to let you know, that's a true snug mug!"

The shady oaks sway with a chuckling glee,
"Come join us, folks, for a fun jubilee!"
With acorns falling like silly little balls,
We laugh until it echoes through forested halls.

So gather your friends, let the laughter flow,
In the arboreal haven, where joy tends to grow.
For in this symphony, quiet yet bright,
The trees tell tales till the fall of the night.

Aria of the Earth's Embrace

Beneath the big sky where the wildflowers sprawl,
The earth hums a tune, a whimsical call.
With each wobbly step on the path overgrown,
A sprightly old tortoise claims his throne!

The daisies throw shade at a passing bee,
"Is that pollen you've got, or just some debris?"
In the quiet, the giggles rise high,
Even the clouds wear a hilarious sigh.

As the brook bubbles softly with laughter so pure,
A fish swims by, slick and sure.
"Any catch of the day?" the reeds chime in,
"Just that ticklish tick! It's a wave from the fin!"

So let the heart dance in the earth's warm embrace,
Where humor and nature find their own space.
In every meadow, a chuckle awake,
An aria of life, all silliness at stake!

The Language of Leaves

Beneath the boughs, they chatter bright,
A tumble of leaves in playful flight.
They gossip of squirrels, dapper and bold,
And whisper of secrets that never grow old.

The breeze adds a chuckle, a giggle or two,
As acorns exchange their best jokes, who knew?
Branches sway with laughter, what a splendid scene,
Nature's own jesters, so merry and keen.

Rustling pines tell tales of mischief at dusk,
Of rabbits in sneakers, and porcupines' husk.
Oh, how they relish each prank in the air,
With laughter rippling, a joyful affair.

So next time you wander, just stop for a while,
Listen close to the leaves, they'll share a good smile.
In the dance of the branches, you might just find,
A knowing nod, and a giggle combined.

Conversations with the Wind

The wind pulls a prank on a wandering hat,
Twirling it round, oh, imagine that!
It snickers through branches, a soft little tease,
Tickling the trees with a gentle, soft breeze.

Fluffy clouds join in, they bounce in delight,
Playing hide and seek, oh what a flight!
A puff of a breeze, and a tumble, then swoosh,
The whole sky erupts in a giggling whoosh.

With a gust, it confesses, 'I tickled the brook!'
'And ruffled the feathers of that sleepy rook!'
Whispers of laughter swirl high and low,
As the wind shares its stories, with a whimsical flow.

So trust in the wind, for it carries the fun,
In every soft whisper, there's laughter begun.
With each playful gust and the swirls it bestows,
You'll find joyful tidings where the breezes do blow.

Phrases Floating on Sunbeams

Sunbeams sneak in with a bright, sunny grin,
Giggling and shimmering, let the fun begin.
They bounce on each leaf, and dance on the ground,
Mixing up phrases that twirl all around.

"Catch me if you can!" a glimmering ray chimes,
"Let's play peek-a-boo with the tall, twisting vines!"
From flowers that bloom, to the petals that flutter,
They stitch up a quilt of bright, silky utter.

A dandelion puff bursts with a cheer,
Spreading its laughter, everyone near.
They whisper a tune of the joy that they share,
In the vibrant embrace of the sun's golden glare.

So next time you wander on a warm, sunny day,
Listen for laughter in a bright, radiant way.
For phrases of joy float on bright, gleaming beams,
Inviting us all into whimsical dreams.

Murmurs in the Glistening Glade

In the glade, creatures chatter, with stories to tell,
The rabbits rush past with a giggling yell.
A hedgehog rolls over, quite tickled and round,
While crickets provide a soft, chirpy sound.

A puddle reflects all the glee in a flash,
As frogs croak their punchlines in a splashing bash.
Butterflies laugh as they flutter about,
Painting the air with a twirl and a shout.

"Have you seen the fox? Always late for his meal!"
"Or that silly old owl trying to learn how to wheel?"
The chuckles are plenty, alive in the space,
With glimmers of joy etched on each creature's face.

So wander this glade, where the laughter is sweet,
With each twist and turn, you'll find joy in your feet.
Let the murmurs of merriment guide you and see,
The silly, fun moments that nature can be.

Quatrains in the Shade

Underneath the leafy crown,
Squirrels dance, they twirl and frown.
A raccoon sings a silly song,
Echoing where the shadows throng.

Lizards strike a pose in style,
While crickets chirp with cheeky guile.
The breeze giggles, tickles the trees,
A merry symphony amongst the leaves.

Beetles wear their tiny hats,
Debate the finer points of spats.
A lazy cat naps on a branch,
While ants prepare a grand old dance.

What tales do rise from branches high,
With honeyed laughs and buttered pie?
In the shade, the world's a jest,
Every creature knows how to jest.

Nature's Secret Scrolls

In the green, a whisper flows,
Tales of tickles, giant toes.
Butterflies trade secrets quick,
While dandelions play a trick.

A wacky frog with a bowtie,
Sips on nectar, oh so spry.
His pals puff up, thinking they're grand,
With plans to launch a marching band.

Bees hold meetings in the blooms,
Debating dizzy, buzzing fumes.
A turtle's voice is slow but wise,
Telling jokes 'neath sunny skies.

Nature scribbles in a dance,
Chaos ruled by chance and glance.
Amongst the hide and seek of fun,
The laughter can't be outdone.

Metaphors of the Thicket

In brambles deep, a jest is found,
With goofy trees that twist around.
Foxes giggle, causing a stir,
Taking turns to bait a blur.

A hedgehog dons a clever hat,
While rabbits giggle at that act.
The shadows cloak a playful hare,
Who bets on mushrooms hiding there.

A brook babbles, mischief unfolds,
Fish gossip tales that never grow old.
Each ripple a chuckle, each wave a grin,
A splash of delight as they dive in.

The thicket's filled with metaphors,
As creatures tumble through the doors.
In such a wild, laughing spree,
Every moment's pure comedy.

Cadence of the Cascading Leaves

Leaves tumble like laughter in wind,
Mischief mixed as nature grinned.
A dandy duck takes on the stream,
Debating rafts in a floating dream.

An old owl cracks a silly pun,
As fireflies flicker, join the fun.
A dance-off starts amidst the ferns,
With every twirl, the humor churns.

Grasshoppers leap, their legs a blur,
While toads try their luck at a purr.
The sun paints smiles on all it sees,
While vines weave tales of breezy ease.

In the rustle of the panoramic stage,
Each leaf a voice, blithe and sage.
Cascading echoes fill the glen,
Where laughter lingers—come again!

Crafted Sentences Amongst the Fronds

In a forest where the trees conspire,
A squirrel took an unexpected flyer.
He tried to send a letter to the moon,
But misplaced the stamp, oh what a boon!

A rabbit read the notes with glee,
Tales of acorns and a shady spree.
He chuckled loud, fell into a hole,
Words made him tumble, now that's the goal!

A wise old owl kept a curious eye,
On the silly chatter as they passed by.
He hooted softly, slow and profound,
While a leaf took flight, spinning around.

Nature's laughter rang through the leaves,
As vines danced along with gossip and thieves.
The trees were whispering tales so grand,
In this leafy realm, the fun was unplanned!

Figurative Language of the Forest Floor

Beneath the fronds where creatures dwell,
A hedgehog shared a tale, oh so swell.
The mushrooms giggled, the ferns turned bright,
As words took flight in the warm sunlight.

A crow cawed puns from the high-up boughs,
While ants debated, in their bustling vows.
"Let's throw a dinner, just us and the toads!"
Chirped a cricket, ignoring the codes.

With similes gliding like leaves in the breeze,
They wove little stories with giggles and tease.
Metaphors grew like wildflowers' bloom,
In this bustling plot, there was always room.

The grass tickled feet, laughter floated wide,
As nature joined in for the whimsical ride.
Simmering voices beneath the green shade,
Wove together choruses, never to fade!

Verbiage in the Wildflower Meadow

In a meadow bright where daisies prance,
A butterfly wrote a verse in a dance.
He flapped his wings, inked with the sun,
Announcing his poems, oh what fun!

The daisies, they giggled, making a fuss,
As bumblebees buzzed with mischievous cuss.
They sipped the sweet nectar, dropped little rhymes,
While ants marched on, making silly crimes.

A ladybug rolled with laughter too loud,
While sunbeams warmed up the curious crowd.
They jotted down jokes on petals so soft,
As poetry grew, they looked on aloft.

In this vibrant spot, they shared their delight,
With playful banter from morning till night.
In the wildflower meadow, joy found its voice,
In chatter and giggles, all danced by choice!

Tapestries of the Tangled Underbrush

In the underbrush deep where shadows lie,
A hedgehog spun tales that soared up high.
With tangled twigs, he crafted a plot,
Of a squirrel who wanted to be a robot.

The vines all leaned in, curious and bold,
To hear of the antics in stories retold.
A mouse with a cap served nutty delight,
While the frogs played harmonicas through the night.

Caterpillars chuckled, weaving their dreams,
In this bizarre patch, nothing's as it seems.
Through giggling whispers and rustling leaves,
Tangled up in laughter, the forest believes.

In this vibrant chaos, joy wove a thread,
Creating a tapestry where worries fled.
With every sneaky giggle and plenty to share,
The underbrush flourished with humor in air!

Cadences of the Coiling Vines

In the garden of giggles, a squirrel runs by,
Whispering secrets to the leaves up high.
The vines twist and turn, a playful tryst,
They tickle the air with every twist.

A rabbit declares, with a hop and a grin,
That grass is just hair, on the outside we're thin.
A bug in a suit holds court with a shout,
Claiming the flowers have too many clout.

The breeze joins the laughter, a ticklish tease,
Making petals flutter like a silly sneeze.
Vines coil together, in a dance oh so fine,
While the sun rolls in, to join the divine.

Together they giggle, a humorous sight,
In nature's own theater, full of delight.
Not a worry in sight, just jests all around,
Where laughter and greenery forever abound.

Dialogues between the Dancing Branches

Oh dear, cried the branches, what a day to flail!
Is that a big crow, or a dangerous whale?
They swing left and right, with a chirpy debate,
As the wind giggles, just eager to sate.

A branch says, 'Watch me, I'll do a grand dip!'
But alas! One tight turn, and it starts to slip.
'Hold your bark!' laughs another, in glee so absurd,
While a nearby flower gives a witty word.

'What's in the trees?' asks a curious bee,
'Just dance and don't buzz, you'll get lost like me!'
The leaves break into laughter, as shadows grow long,
Composing a chorus, an accidental song.

With each twist and twirl, the forest comes alive,
In playful discussions, all frisky to thrive.
No serious banquet, just jests tossed in air,
As the trees draft their plans, for a comical fair.

Lyrics of the Lush Landscape

A meadow sings softly, with a tickle and tease,
Chirping and chirping, echoing unease.
The daisies all chuckle at the grass's green shoes,
As they sway and whimper, chuckling the blues.

"Oh look at that snail, he's got all day!"
Said a leaf to another, in a fun-filled ballet.
Don't hurry, dear snail, this isn't a race,
They laughed until sunlight provided them space.

The butterfly hiccuped, mid-flight as it spun,
Dancing on petals, oh, what a run!
Each flower a stage, every breeze wrote a script,
While cloud bursts of humor were wildly equipped.

Through the lush landscape, the laughter did flow,
With whispers of joy, in the sunshine's soft glow.
The entire world chuckles, in nature's embrace,
As laughter takes root in this beautiful place.

Poetics of the Pristine Pines

Among the tall pines, a gathering was held,
With squirrels as poets, and the wind as their guild.
Each branch shared their wisdom, a joke or a jest,
With giggles and snickers—oh, what a fest!

'What do you call it, when a pine starts to dance?'
Asked one little pine, giving fate a glance.
'A nutty performance!' quipped back with a cackle,
While the owls looked down, feigning their crackle.

A raccoon with brilliance, a top hat in tow,
Declared he could juggle, the seeds in a row.
The pines did their best, to stifle their snorts,
As he wobbled and fumbled, like a jester in shorts.

Underneath boughs weaving, the laughter rang out,
With shadows engaged in a light-hearted bout.
The pristine pines whisper, in rhythms so bright,
Welcoming humor to dance in their light.

Dreamscapes Under the Canopy

Squirrels debate who's the best,
Chirping songs in a funny jest.
A raccoon's mask hides a cheeky grin,
As he swipes snacks, thinking he'll win.

The breeze plays tricks on their tails,
Rustling leaves like old fairy tales.
A snickering owl hoots with delight,
As fireflies dance, glowing at night.

Mistakes are made, like missteps in dance,
Bumblebees buzzing, they take a chance.
Giggling frogs jump from lily to leaf,
Creating chaos, bringing relief.

Together they play, in laughter they bask,
In secret whispers, they dare to ask.
The humor within the rustling green,
Makes the wild heart feel truly seen.

Vignettes of Nature's Brush

A beaver builds while cracking jokes,
Nearby, the rabbits share their hoaxes.
One claims he once outran a cat,
While another swears he's part acrobat.

The trees lean in to hear the tale,
While ladybugs giggle, striking a scale.
A butterfly flutters with flair so bright,
Landing on a leaf, she winks with delight.

The wind joins in with a playful sigh,
Tickling branches, making them cry.
Whispers of grass tickle the ground,
As laughter echoes all around.

Every creature, a poet at heart,
Crafting verses like true work of art.
In the vivid canvas, chaos is free,
Nature's laughter, a wild jubilee.

Allegories of the Overgrown

In tangled vines, secrets are spun,
A hedgehog grins, he thinks he's won.
He's built a fortress from twigs and leaves,
While the ants march on, believing he deceives.

A duck quacks loudly, making a scene,
Claiming he's got the best routine.
Friends gather round to witness the show,
But he slips in the mud, his ego just so-so.

The mushrooms chuckle, a wise old crowd,
Spreading old tales, a bit too loud.
Each puffball releases a cloud of fun,
As the sun peeks through, the day's just begun.

At dusk, they gather with twinkling eyes,
Under the stars, where humor lies.
In overgrown patches, life's rhymes unfold,
With laughter and tales, both quirky and bold.

Delicate Dialogues in the Thicket

In the thicket deep, a chat takes flight,
A deer and a rabbit share tea at night.
With cups made of acorns, they sip and sigh,
Over stories of moons that skim the sky.

Crickets chirp while the toads serenade,
With witty quips that never seem to fade.
A porcupine rolls, in laughter he walls,
While near the bushes, a squirrel recalls.

Each rustle of leaves, a punchline clear,
As the night air fills with their playful cheer.
Nature's own stage where creatures collide,
With each dialogue, silly confides.

In shadows they whisper with giggly tones,
Creating a laughter that's all their own.
Through delicate moments, wonder will bloom,
In the heart of the thicket, humor finds room.

Fables in the Forgotten Glade

In a glade where chatter grows,
Squirrels debate the best of toes.
A raccoon's tale spins round and round,
While frogs judge jokes with leaps and bounds.

The breeze whispers secrets, or so they say,
But birds sing loudly to shoo it away.
The trees nod sagely, what a jest!
As crickets play cards, who's clearly the best?

A wise old owl joins in the fun,
With riddles that shine like the mid-day sun.
"Why did the chicken cross the street?"
To find a good laugh—what a treat!

The fireflies giggle, lighting the night,
As laughter dances, a pretty sight.
In the glade where fun takes flight,
Fables are spun till the morning light.

Sonorous Shadows of the Hidden Grove

In the shadows where giggles thrive,
A hedgehog tap dances, quite alive.
The trees sway low, a secret sock,
As rabbits play hopscotch on old rocks.

A parrot squawks with tales to share,
While bats hang upside-down without a care.
They fashion capes from autumn leaves,
And make tall hats from flowers that weave.

The mushrooms giggle, a fungi brigade,
Plotting pranks in the sun and shade.
"Knock, knock!" says one, "Who's there?"
"We're just a bunch without a care!"

Even the breeze joins in to play,
Whirling about in a merry ballet.
In these shadows where laughter lives,
The grove holds secrets only it gives.

Lyrical Contemplations in Nature's Nook

In the nook where quirks make sense,
Hares discuss their fluffy defense.
The daisies gossip, petals afloat,
While a turtle shares tales from his boat.

"Did you hear about the bee so bold?"
"Buzzed into dinner, a feast to behold!"
They laugh at the skunk, what a sight,
Who thinks he can dance—oh, what a fright!

The willows sway with a knowing grin,
Holding the secrets of all that's been.
A lizard in shades, strutting so fine,
Declares, "I'm the prince, and this spot is mine!"

As shadows stretch and the sun bids adieu,
Nature hums softly, a tune tried and true.
In this nook of laughter and cheer,
Life sways to rhythms that draw us near.

Riddles Wrapped in Greenery

Among the leaves with laughter loud,
The frogs tell riddles to gather a crowd.
"Why do ducks swim with their friends?"
"To quack about life and make amends!"

A fox in a hat spins tales quite tall,
While the owls just hoot, "You'll catch your fall!"
The petals curl up with giggly glee,
And the bushes muzzled, whisper, "Not me!"

The sun winks through, a curious sight,
Casting shadows that dance with delight.
Grasshoppers leap, behind the green,
In a world where humor reigns supreme.

The thickets chuckle, a secret shared,
As laughter fills the air, brightly bared.
In a game of wits, the woodland plays,
A riddle unravels in sunbeam rays.

Tales of the Woodland Echo

In the forest where whispers play,
Squirrels debate about nutty day.
Frogs wear hats, oh what a sight,
They leap and croak till the fall of night.

A rabbit's joke brings laughter wide,
As shadows dance on nature's tide.
With berries stolen, a treasure trove,
The critters giggle, they're in the grove.

The owls hoot with a hint of cheer,
Are they wise, or just sipping beer?
Every creature joins the jest,
In this woodland, they'll never rest.

So gather round, let the forest ring,
With tales of mischief and the joy they bring.
In this lush drama, under leafy beams,
Hilarity thrives in their wildest dreams.

Rhymes Beneath the Green Overhead

Under leafy canopies, the squirrels sing,
With acorns bouncing, oh what a fling!
Ladybugs tap dance on blades of grass,
While ants plot mischief, trying to pass.

The bumblebees buzz with their funky beat,
As the flowers sway, they can't be beat.
The hedgehogs giggle at their prickle pride,
In this silly symphony, they all abide.

Silly turtles race in a hilarious crawl,
Betting on the outcome, will they take a fall?
With chirps and squeaks, they cheer and shout,
Beneath the green canopy, joy is about.

So join the fun, in laughter's embrace,
In rhyme and rhythm, we find our place.
From joyful grins to nature's jest,
Under the trees, we are truly blessed.

Thoughts Dancing in Nature's Embrace

Beneath bright skies, where the daisies sway,
Thoughts dance lightly, chasing clouds away.
A puppy prances, tail wagging high,
While butterflies flit, oh my, oh my!

The chipmunks chatter, stories they weave,
Of acorn adventures, you won't believe!
A wily fox plays hide and seek,
In shades of laughter, all creatures peek.

The pond reflects a comical grin,
As frogs wear crowns and declare a win.
The dragonflies twirl in a daring flight,
Chasing the sun into the night.

So let's spin tales under nature's charms,
With giggles and joy, in each other's arms.
In this embrace of life and delight,
We'll dance in the shadows, from morning to night.

Sonnet of the Swaying Grasses

The grasses sway, with secrets untold,
As wind spins yarns of the brave and bold.
A prankster lizard does a little jig,
While crickets strum on a tiny twig.

The tall pine trees chuckle with glee,
As shadows play tag, just wait and see!
A group of toads form a singing band,
With a splashy beat, they take a stand.

The bloom of jest spreads on every side,
As daisies wink, feeling the pride.
Through swaying greens, laughter takes flight,
In nature's harmony, spirits ignite.

So gather the sunbeams and dance along,
In the grassy arena, you can't go wrong.
With each silly step, let joy emanate,
In the sway of the grasses, life feels great.

Whispers in the Wistful Grove

In the grove where squirrels chat,
Rabbits giggle, imagine that!
They play hide and seek with glee,
While butterflies dance, wild and free.

A chatty breeze tickles the leaves,
"Stop that tickling!" the tree believes.
The daisies wink and share a joke,
Even the old oak starts to poke.

The sun peeks in with a playful grin,
"Let's all gather and let fun begin!"
The shadows stretch, the laughter swells,
In this grove, there are no farewell bells.

Crickets chirp with a playful beat,
As frogs leap and take to their feet.
In this rhythmic, joyous stride,
Nature's humor cannot hide.

Secrets Beneath the Swaying Boughs

Under branches long and wide,
Creatures gather, side by side.
Chattering squirrels share their snacks,
While wise old owls keep off track.

A fox tells tales of narrow escapes,
As rabbits roll in silly capes.
The leaves above begin to sway,
Joining in on this funny play.

Caterpillars strut with style,
Wiggling just to make us smile.
The trees shake, the bushes giggle,
As worms join in with a wiggly wiggle.

Sunlight filters through the green,
Casting shadows in a lively scene.
In the giggles of the critters' throng,
Nature hums a happy song.

Echoes of Leaves in Quietude

In hush, the leaves begin to sing,
Telling tales of Winter's fling.
A mouse shimmies, trying to dance,
While turtles take their slow advance.

The whispers tease, a breeze so sly,
Promising fun but telling lies.
The acorns roll, a game unfolds,
With giggles shared, their humor bold.

Sunbeams flicker like laughing eyes,
As frogs croak out their silly cries.
The woodpecker joins in with a tap,
Nature's jesters in a playful nap.

Underneath the sprawling trees,
Laughter echoes in the breeze.
In quietude, the joy's immense,
A world where seriousness makes no sense.

Verses Beneath the Verdant Canopy

Under canopies lush and green,
A bustling crew can always be seen.
Mice wear hats, the raccoons play,
As the world swirls in a funny ballet.

The sun breaks through with a wink,
Bringing forth a twist and pink.
With raindrops tapping on leaves so light,
A dance-party forms, what pure delight!

Frogs jump high with a boom and plop,
While butterflies flutter and never stop.
Each flower shares a secret or two,
About the antics they all pursue.

Shadows play hide and seek at dusk,
Perfecting mischief; oh, how we trust!
Beneath the branches' playful shade,
Laughter lingers, memories made.

Imagery of the Untamed Meadow

In fields so wild, a goat took a stroll,
Wearing a hat, oh so comic and whole.
It paused and it posed for a curious mouse,
Who chuckled aloud in its tiny little house.

A squirrel danced wildly, its tail in the air,
While birds dropped their snacks, without any care.
The flowers all giggled, their petals they'd wave,
As the bee lost its way in a sugar-filled cave.

A cow tried to jump and got stuck on a fence,
With a mooo of embarrassment, oh what a tense!
The setting sun rolled, a giant pumpkin pie,
And the wind whispered jokes as it danced on by.

So here in this meadow, where laughter runs free,
The animals play games, just as happy can be.
With mischief abounding, let the day carry on,
For life is a hoot, until the last light is gone!

Stanzas within the Foliage

Amidst emerald greens, a rabbit let fly,
With socks on its feet, oh me, oh my!
It tripped on a root, tumbled head over heels,
And the turtles all laughed, sharing their meals.

A fox wore a scarf, looking quite dapper,
Said, "Style is essential!" but gave a loud clapper.
He slipped on some leaves, went into a spin,
Now everyone's giggling, where do I begin?

A wise old owl perched high on a limb,
Told jokes with a twist, sang on a whim.
The deer rolled its eyes, while the raccoons all cheer,
They brought out the snacks—oh, what a great year!

So here in this jungle, where humor is rife,
The creatures find joy in this whimsical life.
With laughter like thunder through branches so grand,
In nature's own theatre, the fun has been planned!

Prose Beneath the Starry Canopy

Under twinkling stars, a badger made stew,
Called friends to the feast, the raccoon and crew.
The pot boiled over, what a sight to behold,
With veggies a-flying, stories untold.

A turtle brought salsa, a cat brought some cheese,
The owl hooted loudly, "Kick it up, please!"
So they danced round the fire, in the middle of night,
With shadows doing jigs, what a fantastic sight!

The moon looked amused, offering light with a grin,
As laughter erupted from every thick skin.
The night stretched and yawned, with giggles in tow,
While fireflies joined in with their soft, glowing glow.

Here in this moment, 'neath celestial beams,
The joy is infectious, igniting their dreams.
With fun in the air, let the antics unfold,
For beneath these bright stars, the stories are gold!

Fragments of Fables in the Forest

In the heart of the woods, a frog wore a crown,
Proclaimed himself king with a leap and a bounce.
But every straight jump made him land in a puddle,
As the critters all giggled, giving him trouble.

A bear with a cape tried to fly like a kite,
With a swoosh and a swish, he took off with delight.
But he wobbled and tumbled, and down he did crash,
All the chipmunks snickered, a brightening splash!

A wise old porcupine told tales of the past,
But his quills were so sharp, nobody sat fast.
With each funny fable, they rolled on the ground,
Between fits of laughter, true joy could be found.

So here in this haven, where humor runs deep,
The animals gather, their laughter to keep.
In fragments of fables, spun wild through the trees,
They find in each moment, a life filled with ease!

Fables in the Forest's Heart

In the woods where squirrels dance,
A raccoon tried to steal a glance.
But tripped on roots, fell with a plop,
The laughter echoed, never did stop.

The owl wore glasses, far too bright,
Claimed he could read both day and night.
He squinted hard, all pages flew,
And landed right in a bat's shoe!

A fox, quite clever, baked a pie,
But burnt it crisp, oh me, oh my!
The forest critters laughed and cheered,
As they all said, "Let's eat the weird!"

A turtle raced in a wooden boat,
His finish line? A floating moat!
But took a nap half-way, you see,
Dreamt of a prize, maybe some tea!

Timbered Tales of Timelessness

Beneath the boughs of a mighty tree,
A frog held court, a king, quite free.
With a crown of leaves, he croaked with pride,
"Who needs a throne when you've got stride?"

A hedgehog wrote a comedy play,
In spiky costumes for the big day.
The audience roared, they could barely breathe,
As laughter rustled the autumn leaves.

The badger donned a shiny dress,
Claiming it was a grand success.
But slipped on dew, oh what a sight,
He twirled so fast, then flew in flight!

A caterpillar with dreams so bold,
Told of adventures yet untold.
"Just wait," he said, "I'll soon turn spry,
And dance through the air, oh me, oh my!"

Notes from the Nestled Nook

The chipmunks had a talent show,
With tiny acts, a comedic flow.
One juggled nuts, oh how they flew,
While another sang, "I love my stew!"

A beaver built a bridge of jokes,
But all it did was stun the folks.
With puns and pouts, he made quite a splash,
As they laughed hard, he blushed in a flash.

The woodpecker drummed a funny beat,
As woodland friends twirled on their feet.
They joined in chorus, a merry sound,
Echoing joy through the nature-bound.

When twilight came, they shared the tales,
Of silly quests, and wild gales.
As stars peeked through the tangled bough,
They giggled loud, "Let's do it now!"

Syllables in the Shaded Sanctuary

In a nook where shadows play,
A wise old goat had much to say.
"Do you think I'm just a fool?
Well, I'm the king of this old school!"

A rabbit wore a polka dot tie,
Claimed it made him look quite spry.
But slipped on mud, oh what a scene,
He became a quagmire machine!

The mice formed a band with acorn drums,
They sang sweet tunes that made hearts hum.
Yet one fell asleep beneath the stage,
And woke to cheers, much to his rage!

A cranky owl hooted late at night,
"Keep it down, it's my nap time plight!"
But giggles turned into a serenade,
His scowl soon faded, fun was made!

Reflections of a Forest Heart

In the shade where squirrels play,
A tree once tried to join a ballet.
It tripped on roots, fell with a thud,
The forest chuckled, "Just a little bud!"

A fox wore glasses, said he could see,
His vision was fine until he met a bee.
"I thought you were honey," he squeaked and ran,
The bees buzzed loudly, "Forget the plan!"

Mushrooms held parties, just past the creek,
But the wise old owl said, "No, that's too bleak!"
The fungi danced wildly, their caps in a spin,
While the owl hooted, "Now this is a win!"

Beneath the stars, the leaves began to sway,
The critters gathered, ready to play.
A well-timed joke made the badgers grin wide,
In this forest heart, joy is the guide.

Musings in the Meadow Mist

The daisies giggle, with laughter so bright,
"Why did the bee stay out all night?"
He needed to buzz with a friend on a whim,
But the moonlight made him feel rather dim.

A rabbit in glasses debated his fate,
"Should I munch on lettuce or steal some cake?"
But the tortoise argued, with wisdom so deep,
"Why rush a dessert? Let's think and then leap."

The grasshoppers chirped, trying to sound cool,
While ants marched along, keeping march like a school.
"Are we lost?" asked one, looking up at the sky,
"Or just perfecting our dance moves? Oh my!"

In the morning glow, as soft mist does rise,
The meadow springs laughter, a joyful surprise.
With tickles from dew, all creatures partake,
In the fun of the meadow, there's never a break.

Epiphanies Within the Greenery

A parrot proclaimed, with feathers all bright,
"Why does a cactus have such a fright?"
It just stood there quiet and shrugged with a frown,
"It's hard to find friends when you're prickly and brown!"

A lazy old bear tried yoga one day,
But he rolled and he tumbled, then flopped in the hay.
"Namaste, my bumble," he panted with glee,
"Maybe tree pose isn't the best fit for me."

In the vines where the laughter flowed like a stream,
A frog declared, "What a curious dream!
I leaped through the clouds, and to my surprise,
The stars were just fireflies in a disguise!"

When crickets held court under twinkling stars,
They debated on life, and who drives the cars.
In a land full of jest, they found out in the end,
It's laughter that truly makes nature a friend.

Syllables of the Soft Wind

The wind played a tune with branches so spry,
"Can you feel the rhythm?" it whispered on by.
A raccoon tried singing, with a curious style,
But the notes came out funny, they made everyone smile.

Dandelions danced, their seeds all aflame,
"Let's blow them away!" they called out in a game.
But the breeze had its plans, it spun them around,
And the seeds flew off, without making a sound.

A chipmunk in spectacles wrote poems in dirt,
About nuts and good berries, and times when he hurt.
"Why can't squirrels share?" he pondered one day,
After figuring out they would rather just play!

The breeze carried laughter through trees to the sky,
As the world joined the dance, with a gleam in each eye.
In this moment of joy under soft whispers' bind,
The forest kept secrets, no one could find.

Legends of Life Laced Leaves

In the breeze, leaves giggle soft,
They whisper tales of trees aloft.
Squirrels dance with acorn hats,
While owls hoot, 'What's up with that?'

Each gust a jest, each rustle a grin,
A comedic skit by nature's kin.
Beneath the boughs, the mischief grows,
As clever roots tickle their toes.

The sunlight spills, like lemonade,
On leafy jesters in masquerade.
Pinecones chuckle, falling down,
"Oh dear, we're wearing nature's crown!"

The wind, a jester, plays its part,
As branches sway with joyous heart.
A chorus of chuckles in the air,
Finding humor everywhere!

Conversations at Dusk's Edge

At dusk, the branches start to chat,
"Did you hear that pun from the cat?"
The crickets laugh and chirp along,
While shadows play their nightly song.

A weasel jokes about the moon,
Claiming it hums a silly tune.
As fireflies flicker, bursting with glee,
They shine like stars on a comedic spree.

"Oh, look!" says one, "the owl's eyes wide,
Do you think they're just really surprised?"
And leaves rustle, sharing their quirks,
Swaying as if with goofy smirks.

Beneath the arch of the dimming sky,
Even the pines seem to sigh and pry.
"Hey, did you see that fox goofing?"
With laughter echoing, no time for snoozing!

Verses from the Voyaging Vines

Through trellises and twirls, they weave,
Vines exchange their antics, believe!
"Did you trip?" one whispers with glee,
"Or was it the wind, making you flee?"

Tangled tales in a viney embrace,
Each twist and turn, a comedy space.
"Grab hold of my humor!" they slyly shout,
As the sunlight dances all about.

They plot their routes, light as air,
"Let's prank the bushes, if they dare!"
Laughter clings, like dew at dawn,
In the garden where jokes are drawn.

A thicket groans with playful sneers,
While daisies giggle, shedding their tears.
What comes next? A leafy play,
As vines encircle and sway away!

Eulogies for the Fallen Leaves

Fallen leaves gather for a grand affair,
"Remember when we danced in the air?"
They rustle their stories, tales of delight,
Of windy waltzes in the warm sunlight.

"Oh dear," says one, in a whisper so low,
"I landed in soup, what a way to go!"
The crowd bursts out in a ribbeting roar,
As memories of mischief begin to pour.

Each leaf shares a giggle, while wrapped in the past,
"Remember the time we were bound to last?"
But humor glistens through every plight,
As they recall their adventures, so bright.

With a laugh and a flutter, they bid adieu,
To the branches above, where the joy always grew.
Eulogies sung with a whimsical feel,
For leaves that once danced, with laughter to seal!

www.ingramcontent.com/pod-product-compliance
Lightning Source LLC
Chambersburg PA
CBHW071827160426
43209CB00003B/223